Rhymes for Lyme

Justin Lindorf

BookLeaf Publishing
India | USA | UK

Presentation by *BookLeaf Publishing*

Web: www.bookleafpub.com

E-mail: info@bookleafpub.com

ISBN: 9789394788978

First edition 2022

DEDICATION

Dedicated to everyone suffering from Lyme disease. My family who helped me get to where I am today. My best friends.

The music that got me through the hardest times.

The doctors who study Lyme and have helped treat me. My mental health therapists. Specifically, Evangeline, Beth, Jacquilynn, Joshua, Terri, Ron, Scott, Bryce, Dustin, Steve, Christian, Cuyler, Eric, Austin, Reagan, Alan, Petersen, Moore, KC, Marcus, TJ, Kosins, Byron, Lisa, Jessie, Waisbren, Omar, Laura, Stacey, Laycee, Kevin, Matthew, Rivers and Marshall and My Real Life Slim Sadie.

Thank you for being in my life and for giving me a reason to never settle and to keep fucking going.

I Know This Fucking Sucks

I just want someone
To ask me how I'm doing
And really mean it
So if there's someone out there
Who is up to the task
Just call, I don't care what time it's at
Justin, why are you so sad?

I don't need anyone else dissing me
I don't need you to be kissing me
I don't need anyone else missing me
I don't need anyone blessing me
I just need to hear
I know this fucking sucks

I just want that connection
Stead of the lectures and the lessons
I don't need your opinion
Of how I can move from sad to glad
I just want you to listen and say
I know this fucking sucks

Don't wish me better luck
Don't tell me I'm just stuck
Just sit there while we sip Starbucks
And say, I know this fucking sucks

When I say I don't know what to do
I don't know where to go
Say it doesn't matter what you do
It doesn't matter where you go
I'll be there with you
I know this fucking sucks

I'll always lend my ear
I'll always love you dear
I can hear the fear

It's in your tone
You don't have to do this alone
I'm right here
I know this fucking sucks

Don't try to save me from my pain
Don't try to restrain me
Don't try to entertain me
All I'm asking is that you say
I know this fucking sucks

Please don't try to fix it
Please don't dismiss it
Please don't say you've got just the ticket
Please just sit and visit and say
I know this fucking sucks

Can't win a battle if there's nothing to be won
Can't lift a rock if it weighs a ton
Can't fire a bullet without a gun
Can't enjoy a burger without a bun
Just want to hear anyone say
I know this fucking sucks

I don't need you to understand
I don't need you to hold my hand
I don't need you to make a plan
I don't need you to take a stand
I just need to hear

I know this fucking sucks

Please don't offer an alternative
Please, your advice, don't give it
Please don't tell me how I should live with it
Please don't be comparative
Please don't tell me to forgive it
All I'm asking is to hear it
I know this fucking sucks

Time Passes

Time passes so fast
It takes life away
Will make this last
I'm here to stay

Don't know what to do
Don't know where to go
Don't know with who
Don't know how to know

Get lost in my thoughts
Retrace every step
Untangle these knots
Or drown in the depth

Where is the light
I need it right now
Put up a fight
And then take a bow

Don't know what to do
Don't know where to go
Don't know with who
Don't know how to know

I'll take a knee
I want some relief
You don't know me
I'll get through my grief

Please change the channel
It's getting old
Please bring my flannel
It's getting cold

Don't know what to do
Don't know where to go
Don't know with who
Don't know how to know

The sun is going down
And the moon is full
Get out of this town
Life is getting dull

Feel my heart beat
Under my chest
This is my heat
I'll do my best

Don't know what to do
Don't know where to go
Don't know with who
Don't know how to know

Lost in this world
Can't find my place
Watch it unfurl
End of a race

Love and support
Lifting me up
Please don't abort
Filling my cup

Don't know what to do
Don't know where to go
Don't know with who
Don't know how to know

Don't know what to do
Don't know where to go
Don't know with who
Don't know how to know

You Will

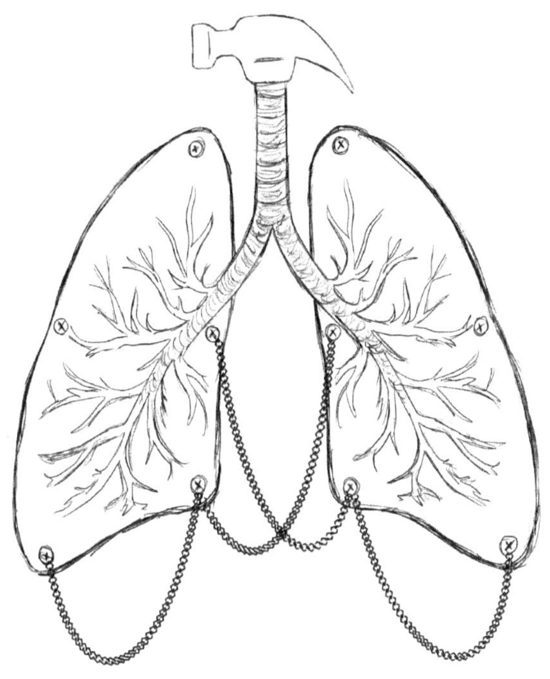

You don't have to tell your lungs to fill

 You don't have to tell your heart to feel

You'll breathe

You will

You'll hurt

You will

You don't have to tell your eyes to tear

You don't have to tell your thoughts to dream

You'll cry

You will

You'll fly

You will

You don't have to tell your ears to hear

You don't have to tell your nerves to steel

You'll listen

You will

You'll fear

You will

You don't have to tell your body to rest

You don't have to tell your ego to die

You'll sleep

You will

You'll humble

You will

You don't have to tell your patience to wait

You don't have to tell your humor to tame

You'll happen

You will

You'll offend

You will

Empathy

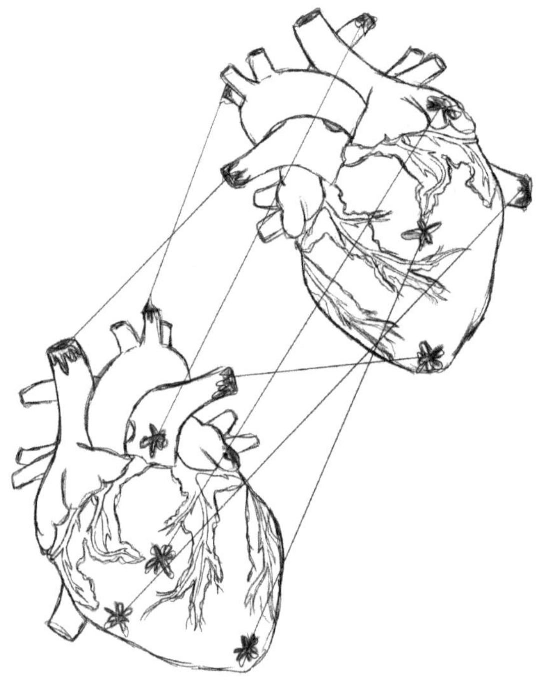

I can feel your tears on my face
I can feel the fear on your face
You know I've been in your place
And I'd do anything to replace
The pain you feel in this state

I'm here for a warm embrace
No judgement not even a trace
Come with me and I'll be your safe place
Even though your scenario is worst-case
Your pain is real there is no debate

Everything in your head I can validate
Those thoughts that you have, they too make me
irate
That happened to me too when I was only eight
None of this is your fault, let's get that straight
This isn't a punishment for your mistakes

In this world there's a lot of hate
For this lack of love, empathy must compensate
When you lift another whose burden is great
For both you and them life becomes easier to
tolerate
So help out, give you both a break

It doesn't matter how you look or what you
make
I'll still love you, for goodness sake
Some things we must forsake
And in other things we must partake
But our relationship is forever safe

Pain and Pride

Flashing through my brain
All the memories of misery and pain
Even indoors, it's cloudy and it rains
I don't know how I will sustain
Living through this much pain
Drugs have been my solution
For my pain, it's dilution
Makes it much less acute

How can anyone accuse me
Of throwing away my life?
When all I'm doing is improving how I feel
Why can't others see how this is so real?
This is just how I deal
With all the unnecessary and unreal
circumstances I've been given,
Can't I just be forgiven?
For what I must have had to do,
To be dealt so much pain, so much distance and
disdain
How can anyone ask me to maintain
A smile?
To falsely contain how much I want to complain
What is possibly to gain by living with so much
pain?
Some say strength,
Well that's a hell of a length
To only gain some strength
To brush big things off like they ain't no thang
If I had a nickel for every time I was told
"You're so strong!"
I'd have enough money to right all the world's
wrongs,
To live happily, lavishly and hopefully for long
Maybe someday I'll even be the subject of a
fight song,
Laughing at my pain when I'm on the other side
Making sure it knew

It had me all wrong,
It underestimated me
It thought it would be the death of me
But in the end, the only thing that died, was my
arrogance and pride
And if that is the strength and lesson I was lucky
enough to learn,
I'd do it two more times, if that is the gift that I
would earn

IDGAF

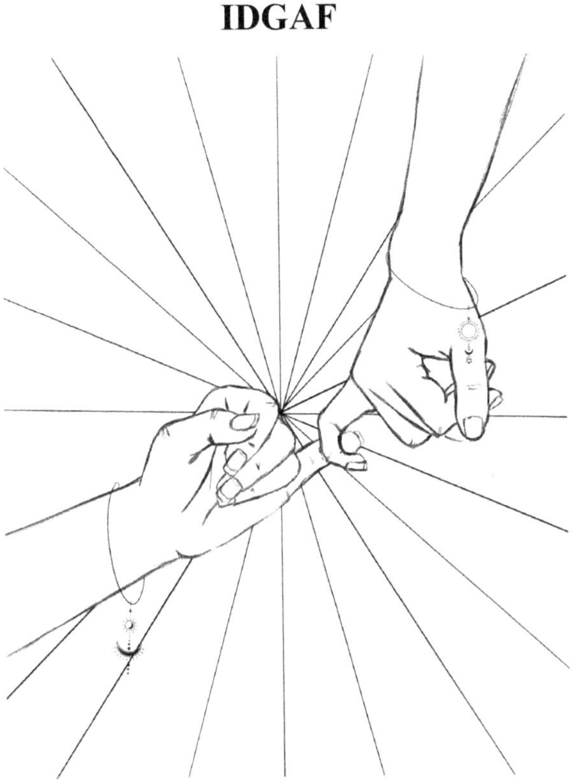

I do give a fuck what you feel and think
Especially about me

We talk
We've walked
We knocked
We shock

How do you see me?
How do you see me?

We flirt
We've sweat shirted
We've mini skirted
We dirt

How do you see me?
How do you see me?

I do give a fuck what you feel and think
Especially about me

We drink
We rethink
We lip sync
We wink

How do you see me?
How do you see me?

We laughed
We cried
We lived
We lied

How do you see me?
How do you see me?

I do give a fuck what you feel and think
Especially about me

We gave
We forgave
We enslaved
We slave

How do you see me?
How do you see me?

We loved
We judged
We shrugged
We hugged

How do you see me?
How do you see me?

I do give a fuck what you feel and think
Especially about me

I would never want my pain or insecurity
To be the reason you are on the brink

Keep Fucking Failing

Keep Fucking Failing

I
Fail, fail, fail,
What in the actual Hell?

I
Wail, wail, wail,

What in the actual Hell?

I
Wait, wait, wait,
What in the actual Hell?

Is this
Fate, fate, fate?
What in the actual Hell?

Am I too
Frail, frail, frail?
What in the actual Hell?

This is like
Jail, jail, jail
What in the actual Hell?

Should I
Bail, bail, bail?
What in the actual Hell?

Never settle down in the dust
Keep Fucking falling short
You can do this, you are from the toughest of the
sort

It's only a permanent failure if you don't get
back up, you must

Even if you have to lie to yourself, omit, or
factually distort
Tell yourself whatever it is that makes it possible
one day to report you won

I failed and failed and failed again,
But I never let that fucking failure win

No Time

There is never enough time
When you're suffering from Lyme
You know you love them
But inside, you are trying to survive ungodly
amounts of mayhem

There is no one else
There isn't even time for yourself

To enjoy anything
Even the person who you are with
It's like the love you had before the Lyme,
Did it even exist?
You both wear a ring but don't know a thing
about each other
And how could you when all you think and see
and hear and feel is different from one another?

Even the ones in your life with whom you share
a mother
They could never even begin to discover,
What it's like inside that broken brain and body
Until they go through something so severe and
spend ninety percent of their time as zombies,
It doesn't even matter that you came from the
same mommy

Your friends, some of those ships will end
Cuz you are always at your wits something or
other,
With your own life
They can kind of feel like you stuck something
in their back
Knife
Especially when you have to cancel for the third
time in two weeks on what used to be your night
Life

Coworkers, just cease to exist
Cuz you can no longer coexist with that thing
you used to love
Work

It hurts

Relationships change
Some ride on, some will die and some will
remain
Some will always stay the same
But it's the forever ride or die
That gives you a reason why
To stay, to remain, to keep tolerating the pain, to
keep existing on, through all the profane
Those are the best people, cuz they are also kind
of insane

Relief

It started with Percocet
Lortab, Norco and Vicodin,
Morphine, codeine and OxyContin
Then Fentanyl, then they cut you off
So Heroin
It's Ne'er a win
In fact, you lose what you'd never choose to lose
Friends, family and happiness

Choices and voices of rationality
It won't discriminate cuz of nationality
Or your previous morality
Controls your behavior in totality
I know it sounds like a generality
But saying that is just a formality
Changes your happy mentality
To sad, do anything to get a bag,
Criminality,
Been so desperate I've huffed soaked rags
Then my mind and body lag

I need my cocaine
It's time to rearrange
The sadness and the pain
I need a break from my brain
Those white lines will lie to you
Those bright times will die in you
Those midnights, they'll ignite, an appetite in
you
I'm hindsight, I wish I could delight
In my own might
Avoid being blinded by the white

The Xanax fixes the panics
Real quick
The Valium sucks the emotions like a vacuum
The Ativan, how is it, that it can
Make me always feel like "I'm the man?"

The klonopin, hell fuckin yeah, now the
numbing is on again
Should I take one more or
Will that be wrong again?
Even if it makes my heart feel strong again
I want the aching to be gone again
Even if it makes my heart feel wrong again
When it wears off, when the numbing is gone
again

I need my Diet Coke, please put some rum in it
Oh alcohol, please make me dumb again
Make me forget, how much I know about
Suffering
Make me forget, how much I've been wondering
Please just smother me, so I stop shivering
Please just cover me, so I stop blubbering
Please just discover me, so I stop missing me
Please just mother me, so I can usher in a
recovery
Fuck it, one more shot
It's comforting

I need that green
Not the paper that runs the American dream
Grass, ganja
Marijuana
Weed, it's what I need
I need it to eat

Weed, it's what I need
I need it to sleep
Mary Jane, herb
Dope
Weed, it's what I need
I need it to cope
Weed, it's what I need
I need it to hope
Pot, reefer
Sticky-icky
Weed, it's what I need
I need it to joke
Weed, it's what I need
I need it to revoke
Bud, chronic
Cannabis
Weed, it's what I need
I need it to understand
Weed, it's what I need
I need it to withstand
Dope, flower
Kush
Weed, it's what I need
I need it to breathe
Weed, it's what I need
I need it to believe
Blunt, joint
Bowl
Weed, it's what I need

I need it to control
Weed, it's what I need
I need it to console
Mind, body and soul

I just want some fucking relief

1 cause of Death

We hear all the time in Lyme
That it is suicide,
I beg to differ
And would like to deliver
Something else for you to consider

Cuz I've lost some lovely Lymies
And have tried to put those losses behind me,

But because some have called them quitters
Just because they pulled the trigger
I can't sit back when I hear that, it makes me so
fucking bitter,
No one who calls them that understands, How
deep their life was in the shitter
Their feelings aren't invalid, they don't make it
up, they aren't emotion counterfeiters

I'd like you to consider that there is no #1 cause
of death for Lymies
There are too many reasons people pull the
trigger,
Agony in the joints
Thoughts that never stop
Racing hearts and POTS
No masseuse able to push hard enough
Trigger point
Muscle spasms, we all have them
Night sweats,
Wake up wet
If we are lucky enough to ever fall asleep
Not even resting when we do
Only in our dreams, can we feel something new,
Then waking up to our nightmare life
Remembering that nothing's right
Freeze or flight and always fight
Migraines that never wane
Endless 10+ level pain

Never having energy to bathe
Stomach churns like a crashing tsunami wave
Always being told we are brave
We know we are,
Any movement feels like an ultra marathon
It's so difficult for me, a guy
That even if my dream girl wanted me to get it
on,
I couldn't even muster the strength
to remove her thong,
Anger and rage,
Like a bat let out of a matchbox cage
Sensitivity,
To everything,
Lights and sound and food and medication and
temperature and texture and time and space and
every single thing that is interlaced,
Depression, the lack of other people's respectful
perceptions
Of us,
Anxiety, how it feels all the time like I'm dying,
Then realizing I'm not
And being pissed, that I still exist
In this,
This state,
That doesn't have words to describe
What we Lymies all inevitably feel inside,
Fatigue,
From chronic suffering

And fighting while we suffer,
Carrying these heavy weights
But not getting any buffer,
Knowing we are so alone even if we have a
lover,
Cuz no one could ever understand,
To some extent, not even other Lymies can
If I had to choose just one thing,
That made me want to end my own suffering
It would be only this,
The loneliness

So suicide is not #1
There isn't even a #1
It's all these things multiplied together,
Amplified every second you deal with all of
them together
For me that was 385 million plus
Where I fantasized of being thrown under a bus,
So no, it's not the number one and I hope you
will consider,
That the causes are all these things and countless
more
Our death is just our medication
Suicide is just the route of administration
To send us off on our permanent vacation

Living Through

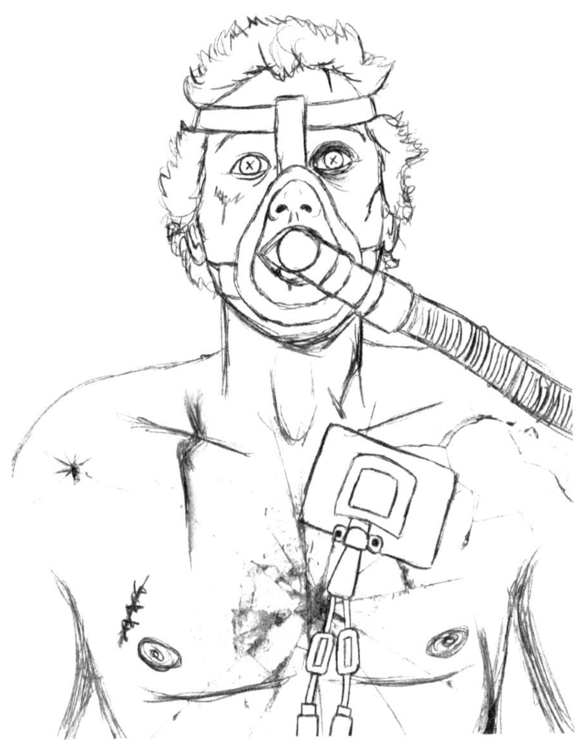

No it wasn't suicide
But I rode my death out like I hadn't died
I lived through it
My own death
No blood, heartbeat or oxygen
But it wasn't my last breath

Standing on top a snowy mountain
One month shy of twenty-five
In the middle of a blizzard, a helicopter flies,
Inside it a young man, beaten, battered and
bruised,
Was finally about to leave his life of chronic
blues,

The helicopter crew would say I technically was
dead,
But they got me to the ICU and revived me in a
bed,

Kidney failure, brain bleed and DKA
My sister a neurologist told my family if I woke,
I would be a vegetable, I wouldn't even know I
used to be a good looking bloke,

My red blood cells had burst, but that's not even
the worst,
I saw my body lying there and watched my
family sob,
I was clearly on the other side but didn't meet a
god,
It was known to me I had a choice
If I wanted to go back all I had to do was nod,
But I didn't know if I could handle being in that
sick bod,

A man who came to help me decide did the only
thing that could make me nod,
He reminded me how much my mom would cry
if I chose not to try,
He hit me with a shovel and told me you're not
trying hard enough,
It pissed me off, but I got up, only to be smacked
down again,
And anyone who knows me, knows I will swing
until the end
I never try less than hard
A hard head is what I am,
And so it goes, all I needed, was to be told my
efforts to survive had just been a fraud

When I woke up all alone with every cavity full
of a tube,
I was scared as hell and couldn't move,
For fifteen minutes, I feared I may have hurt
someone I knew,
Or even worse, some little kid, I didn't have a
clue,
Of how I got there or why,
But, the last thing I remembered was driving
high,
A doc came in and saw my eyes and shouted to
the staff,
He's awake! He's awake!
They and my family all ran in fast

He asked if I could breathe on my own
And I nodded again,
And when they took the tube from my throat I said
"What the FUCK am I doing here again?"

Easy to Catch

And easy to kill,
I believed that until,
I saw every doc with every specialized skill
And still only looked up
Because I only went downhill
Had to drop 2 mill

Even more obscene, is swallowing the pill
That I have swallowed more pills
Than dropped dollar bills,
Yes that's sometimes more than Benjamin's per
day
But they told me that there wasn't any other
way,
To feel better, to get back to life and play,
I would have swallowed and spent ten times
that,
If I had known it was the sure way
To feel better, to get back to life and play

Tens and hundreds and thousands of needles,
IVs, blood draws and false guarantees
From the often pompous and highly degreed,
I don't want to die, but for a while
Non-existence is what I need,
What misdeed did I do to deserve
To feel agony at the end of every nerve?
What greater purpose could this possibly serve?
For anyone? Not just myself
It's hell on earth in and of itself
How does a Lymie relieve oneself?
For too many of us the answer has been,
To end oneself, it's happened again and again

FUCK

Fuck
Fuck fuck fuck
Fuckity fuck fuck fuck
Fuckin fuckers fuckin my life up
Fuckin up my dreams and life
Fuckin up my morning, my breakfast, my
mid-morning and fuckin lunch
Fuckin with my head, my heart and my fuckin
stomach
Fuckin up friendships, just one fuckin tick
Fuckin my health up
Fucked me for a short time
Just to make me fuckin sick
Fuckin forever fatigued
Fuckin my interest for anything
That used to keep me fuckin intrigued
Fuckin up my wants
Now all I want is my fuckin needs
To fuckin sleep
To fuckin eat
To fuckin keep down what I eat
My most basic fuckin human need
To fuck
To fuckin procreate
Now my only fuckin desire is to get fucked up
With fuckin uppers and downers

The drugs never let me fuckin down
Fuckin up my shits, they are rarely brown
Fuckin up my smile, now it's a frown
Fuckin up my living, now I'm a ghost-town
Maybe the only thing it hasn't fucked
Is the most fuckin perfect common noun
I don't give a FUCK now
I don't give a FUCK how
I don't give a FUCK why this is allowed
It's not fuckin okay
To fuckin feel this way
But now I have found I don't give a FUCK
somehow
And that is not even fuckin close to the end of
my list of fuckin fucks
But I'm fuckin done and
Now I'll take a fuckin bow

Ryan

To my dearest Ryan
I promise to keep on trying
And fight through all this lying
I'll keep track of time n'
Bring some light into this Lyme n'
I'll keep fucking going
I ain't got no time for dying
I still need you by my side n'
We will both see this ride end
Taking names and kicking asses
Whatever gets results the fastest
I'll wear as many hats as
The end result requires,
Full throttle, I'll be squealing tires
I won't stop, even though I'm tired
I won't stop, even when I retire
To fight these evil men who conspired
To openly call us liars
In circumstances so dire,
When we met you were on fire
With such a burning desire
I could see the work make you perspire
To save even just one soul
Whose mind and body had taken a toll,
I wish I could have held that trigger I would
have pushed instead of pulled,

Now it's time for you to push and pull
Me, in the right direction
I've had some time for reflection
Every time I think about a different section
Of my life you've made an impact on
I know you are truly a brother that I added on
To my family that I've chosen
I hope you've been released, from some of your
woes,
This goes without saying because I know that
your heart knows,
I will never judge you, never hold a grudge
against you,
I don't understand all of your pain
I wish I did as I stare out my hospital room
window,
I know we just met but my life you have
changed
Now I have hope again that life will continue to
change
I feel like our soldiers are getting within range
To take out some of our enemies
I need your wisdom and guidance please
My brain right now is broken, I'm buckling at
my knees
The train I'm on is smoking, I'm struggling
pretty please
I'll make sure your work lives on
It's something that the whole world needs

I'm sorry that I didn't recognize your needs
I hope that in the future I'll be able to see the
signs with ease,
To stop someone from pulling, who has our
same disease
We're going to win this war in the end,
Offer me your hand to lend
Sit with me in every foxhole
On the frontline of every single battle
When I fall, help me back on my saddle
Your burning desire, under me has lit a fire
I'm pissed, I'm sad, I'm lost, confused and
wired
Even though we both lived and loved with
trauma,
Sometimes our pasts made us feel unloveable,
even by our own mamas
And Hell, we lived through it, Lyme
I'll keep my eyes and ears open to offer help to
your babies and their mama
Whenever they wanna
Ask questions, chat or bitch
I'll try to repair and stitch
Every wound left open by this
Just show me when and how,
Plant the seeds in my brain now
I'll do the work and plow,
Lyme needs us right now,
I felt you comfort me

It was so comforting
I beg you'll continue to lead
and inspire me
Even from the other side
We can still together ride
Through this rollercoaster of why's
When it is all over, we can finally have, our
relieving sighs

Rage

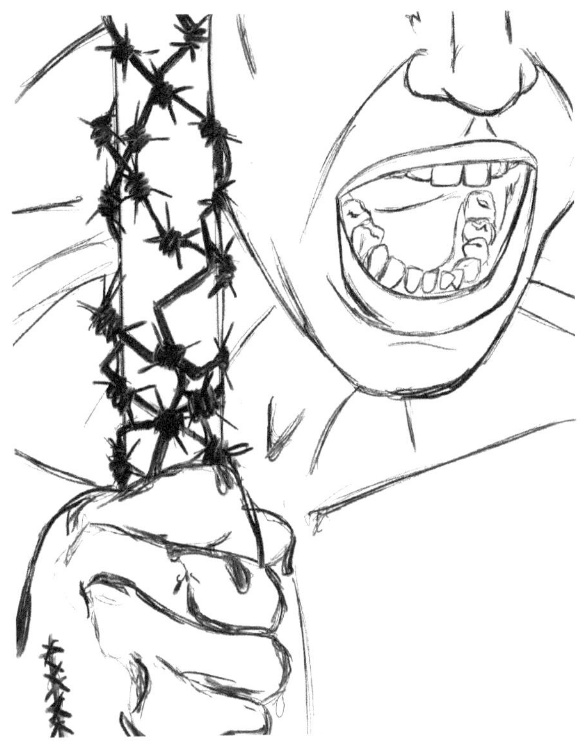

I feel like every aspect of me
Is trapped in a cage
Why do I have to be
Imprisoned at such a young age

Mentally
I'm never broken
Exhausted though, enraged
Disbelief for sure, but it seems like fate has
spoken

Emotionally
I may never heal
Scarred and scared forever more
Alone in this world of surreal

Physically
A centenarian, at only 25
Destined to ache and suffer, for years
No end in sight, I only survive

I don't live

I exist

Endless

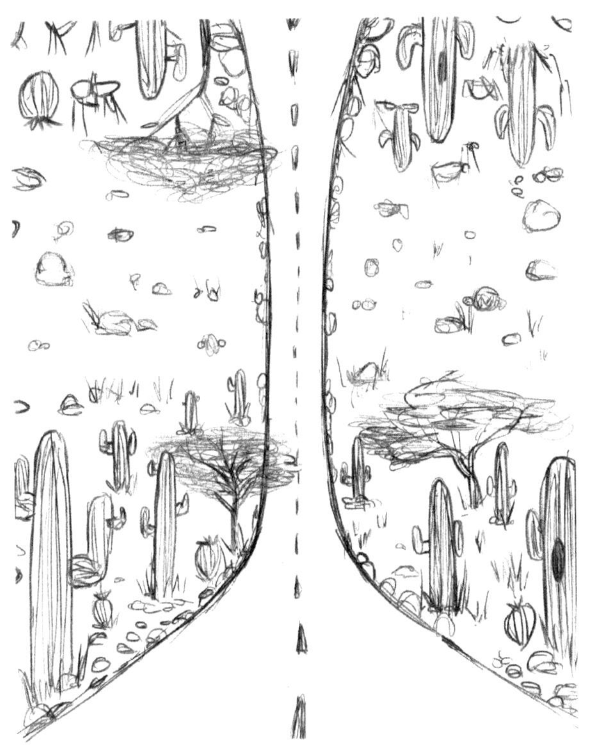

Fears
Tears, doubt,
Burnout, weakness, struggle
Troubles, agony, misery, pressure
Displeasure, rage, hate, insomnia, anxiety

Calamity, heartache, depression, loss, stagnancy,
sadness
Madness, jealousy, envy, anger, contempt,
disbelief, pain
Profane, wants, needs, appointments, scares,
fails, medicine, pills
Uphills, feels, emotions, cancellations, misses,
fatigue, hopes, dreams, nightmares
Despairs, negativity, discomfort, desires,
cravings, withdrawals, gnashing, harassment,
disasters, aches
Mistakes, told-you-so's, sorry's, drugs, nausea,
migraines, dizziness, bathrooms, enemies, cost,
heat

Endless defeat

Unapologetic

Crack
Dark jokes

Cuss
A lot

Cry
It's needed

Sleep
You're tired

Yell
You're pissed

Mourn
You've lost

Grieve
They're missed

Laugh
It's funny

Eat
You're hungry

Question
It's confusing

Thank
Be grateful

Dream
It's possible

Numb
It's hurting

Talk
You'll feel

Feel
You'll heal

Never apologize for what you have to do to
survive

That would be a lie

No one would be happy if you die

How

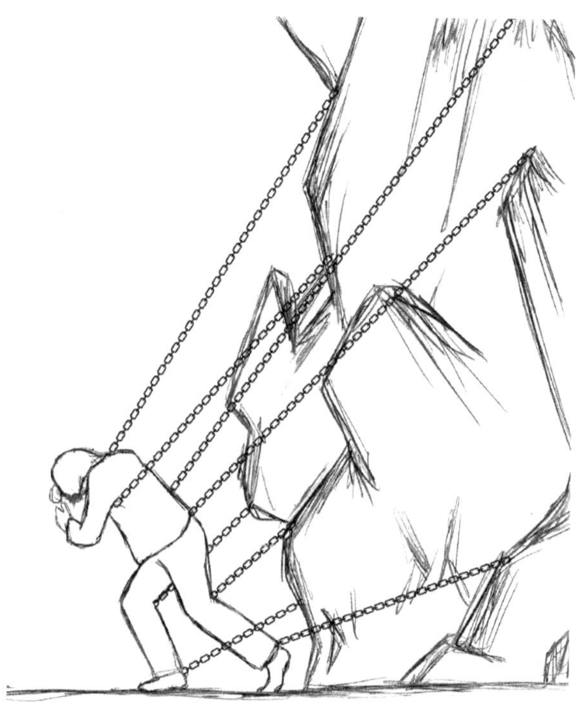

Don't tell me you understand

How could you?

Even I don't

Don't pretend to know

How could you?

Until you do

Don't act sympathetic

How could you?

You haven't even asked what it's like

Don't tell me I'm looking better

How could you?

You haven't even seen me in person

Don't tell me your sob story

How could you?

While you're watching me exist in the middle of
mine

Don't pray for me

How could you?

When you won't even stay by me

Don't admire my strength

How could you?

When you can't know how heavy my weights
are

Don't ask for forgiveness

How could you?

When you aren't changing what I'm asked to
forgive

Don't be upset with me when I cancel plans

How could you?

You know I don't have a choice

Don't tell me you're jealous I don't have to
work

How could you?

When you don't have to work either, you GET
to

Don't speculate

How could you?

When you haven't even asked me why?

Don't hate me

How could you?

When you haven't even tried to relate

Don't forget about me

How could you?

After all we've been through

Don't laugh at me

How could you?

I know my capabilities are less

It's not mine or anyone else's fault

Respect me and what I'm living through

And if you must pray

Pray that you'll never truly understand

I hope you never do

Fake

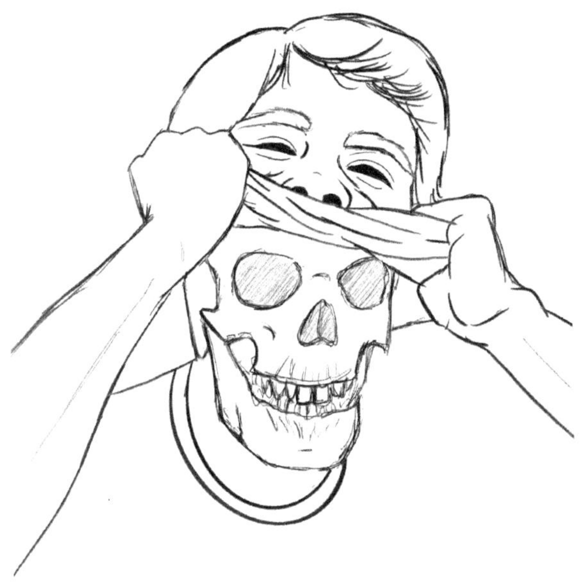

You don't look sick

You're lucky it's treatable

Be glad you don't have cancer

My cousin had that and he can work overtime

What trauma? You have had an incredible life,
you are so lucky

Hypochondriac

If you'd just try harder

I was miserable for a long time too, then I woke
up one day and had enough, now I choose to be
happy, why don't you try that?

That's just from a bug bite right? Can't be that
bad

What do you mean you can't walk?

You don't eat very much

You'd feel better if you exercised

You'd be a new person if you showered
everyday

Essential oils healed my chronic pain, you
should order some from me

I wish I could get massages every week

I would love binging Netflix all day

Let's get you out of bed and go for a walk

You should be less cynical

Don't curse so much

Just think positively

Are you actually taking all your medication?

You're an adult, life is hard, we all have to do things we hate doing

Don't be so dramatic

Attention whore

Freeloader

Stop dwelling on it

Do you ever talk about anything else?

Why didn't you come to the party?

You shouldn't have dropped out of school

Stop smoking, you'll feel better

Drinking won't help anything

Try keeping a journal

You should take more probiotics

Have you ever considered becoming vegan? It healed my stomach

Why don't you just work a few hours a day, you know, part-time?

What about online school?

Start speaking positively

Smile more, cry less

Tough it out, you can do anything you put your mind to!

So and so said you're doing better

You just need to get out of the cold, take a vacation to the beach or something, that helps me reset

Practice gratitude

Count your blessings

It could be worse

At least your family has money

If you wouldn't have stopped going to church

Are you following your doctor's orders?

Why are you so tired?

Why are you so sad?

Why are you so irritated?

Why are you so mad?

If there's ever anything I can do

I wish I could, but…

Have you tried sitting in a sauna?

You're too young to….

Must be nice to do nothing all day

Fake it till you make it

It Exists

A hug is just a hug, until you find the one you're always thinking of

Holding hands is just holding, until you find the one that fits like a glove

A kiss is just a kiss, until you find the one you love

Romance is just a dance, until you have no plans
and meet someone through a game of chance

Dating is just moving your pawns and knights in
shining armor, until she comes in as your queen
and starts checkmating

Missing someone is just reminiscing, until your
heart can not continue in their absence to keep
ignoring and dismissing

Butterflies are just caterpillars, until their cocoon
is opened by a passer-by

A hello is just the beginning of a goodbye, until
you find the one that you'll stand by

Your life has a shelf-life, until you meet the one
who makes you hope for an afterlife

The dark is just a question mark, until you meet
the one who lights up every landmark with her
spark

A daydream is just a nightmare, until you meet
someone who makes you see your biggest
fantasy, is smaller than your new reality

Insecurity is just that, it's not secure,
until you find your person who appreciates and
accepts your vulnerability

Love is just infatuation, until you find the one
you could never create in your own imagination

Then it is true, and it's one heaven of a ride

Never Settle

Keep fucking going
Never stop until you get it,
What you want

Keep fucking going
Never drop until you get it
What? Your health

Keep fucking going
Never swap until you get it
What? Your dream

Never settle for less
Don't stress so much
Every step is progress

Never settle for less
Don't doubt yourself
Ask out the girl of your dreams

Never settle for less
Don't give up yet
Have a sweat it out mindset

Keep fucking going
Never settle
You will die eventually
Make sure it's when there is nothing left
In a Fight? Go down swinging

Keep fucking going
Never settle
You will die eventually
Make sure it's when there is nothing left
Solo? Lose your voice singing

Keep fucking going
Never settle
You will die eventually
Make sure it's when there is nothing left
A quiz? Lose your mind thinking

Never settle
Never stop, you'll get it

Never settle
Never drop, you'll heal

Never settle
Never swap, you'll achieve

Keep fucking going
Don't worry, do anything else

Keep fucking going
Don't regret, what if she says yes?

Keep fucking going
Don't quit, what if you get through it?

Please

NEVER SETTLE
No matter what
KEEP FUCKING GOING